DIMENSIONS OF AN ORCHARD

Dimensions
of an Orchard

Dave Margoshes

2010 Black Moss Press

Library and Archives Canada Cataloguing in Publication

Margoshes, Dave, 1941-
    Dimensions of an orchard / David Margoshes.

Poems.
ISBN 978-0-88753-471-3

    I. Title.

PS8576.A647D56 2010   C811'.54   C2010-902245-9

Cover photo: Marty Gervais
Design: Karen Veryle Monck

Published by Black Moss Press at 2450 Byng Road, Windsor,
Ontario, Canada, N8W 3E8. Black Moss books are distributed in
Canada and the U.S. by LitDistCo. All orders should be directed
there.

Black Moss would like to acknowledge the Canada Council for the
Arts for its publishing program. Assistance was also provided by the
Ontario Arts Council this year.

ONTARIO ARTS COUNCIL
CONSEIL DES ARTS DE L'ONTARIO

Le Conseil des Arts | The Canada Council
du Canada | for the Arts

PRINTED IN CANADA

Acknowledgements

Some of the poems in this collection have appeared previously, sometimes in earlier drafts, in various magazines, anthologies, on radio and on television. My thanks to the editors of these magazines (print and on-line): *The Antigonish Review, Arc, Border Crossings, Canadian Literature, Carousel, CV2, Descant, Echolocation, Event, Fieldstone Review, Grain, In media res, Kaleidoscope, The Literary Review of Canada, The New Quarterly, Prairie Fire, Queen's Quarterly, The Society* and *SugarMule;* the editors of these anthologies: *The Common Sky* (Three Squares Press), *Crossing Lines* (Seraphim Editions*), Listening with the Ear of the Heart* (St. Peter's Press), *2,000% Cracked Wheat* (Coteau Books), and *Vintage 1999* (Ronsdale Press); Kelley Jo Burke, the producer of *Gallery* and *SoundXChange* on CBC Radio in Saskatchewan; and Donna Caruso's Incandescent Films for video versions produced and shown on *Life Without Borders* on SCN-TV in Saskatchewan. In addition, my thanks to artistic director Ruth Smillie and dramaturge Marina Endicott at the Globe Theatre in Regina, where some of the poems in the section *Forms of Devotion* were performed as a dramatic sequence.

My thanks also to the Saskatchewan Arts Board, for financial support during the preparation of this manuscript; to the Saskatchewan Writers Guild, which operates writers and artists colonies at St. Peter's Abbey, Muenster, Sask., and Emma Lake, Sask., where many of these poems were written; and to the monks of St. Peter's, whose hospitality and humility are always an inspiration.

Finally, thanks again to Bob Currie for his sharp eye, Sarah St. Pierre for hers, and Marty Gervais.

Dave Margoshes
April 2010

Contents

Forms of Devotion

Arts and Letters

Phases of the Moon

The Beautiful Wives

Forms of Devotion

Writer's block

On the fourth day, God hit a blank.
He'd already created the earth
with its mountains and great seas
and the firmament, the stars
and the sun and moon, though those two
had not yet been fixed in their orbits.
The poles had been conceived
but not yet created, weather was still
a hazy unformed idea in the back
of his mind, the creatures in all
their multitude and variety just sketches
waiting to be fleshed in, the idea of man
not yet even a glimmer in his eye.
And on the fourth morning, God awoke
with his mind as vacant as the heavens
had been before he fashioned the stars.
He took a walk, did tai chi, would have
gone for a swim but the salt water
irritated his skin and he had yet to imagine
the sweet, but nothing helped. Writer's block
had set in with all its cruelty and irony
and there was nothing to do. No music
to listen to, no self-help books to read,
only the great unmapped terrain
of God's own mind, terrible in its vastness
and the chill of its void. Thus was created
the measureless expanse of time and space
through which our feckless world spins, though God
did not yet know it, the idea taking shape
even while he resisted it. As he struggled
to overcome his block, God began to dream
and through the tangled web he thought
he could hear the first stuttering words
of a distant shout.

Adam and Eve consider the garden

The innocent child walks through this world
naked in her life. She goes to school, to the store
at the corner to buy milk, to the playground
where she skates and is untouched. She is
like Eve in the garden before she learns
the secret. She grows and grows within
her bones, like a weed at the edge of the pond.

The experienced man sheds his skin deep
in the woods where no one else goes. He wars
on his neighbour, slays the stag, bays
at the moon. He is both the snake calling
to Eve and Adam awaiting her return. When
she does come back he sees that she has become
more like him. There is an ache in his side.

The man and the woman walk through
the garden with new eyes, seeing shadows
of a life that could have been. Everywhere,
the garden has fallen into disrepair, walls
crumbling, flowers overgrown. From somewhere
deep in the woods comes the longing call
of a bird and they gaze at each other. Always,
there is that ache.

The seventh day

Why was it God stopped? Six days
of labour and then, nothing. So much
done, so much still to be done. He rested
and no one would say he didn't deserve
to, so much brilliance already to his credit.
But it wasn't just a rest. He stood back,
saw that it was good and left the rest
up to its own devices, let Darwin
be his priest. That was cool, things
worked out all right, some good some
bad, just the way they might have
with God's hand. But what was it
that made him turn away after so much
rapt attention? Had he squinted
into the future, seen something he
didn't like? Did he blink?

At the abbey

Brother Andrew, Brother John
weeding carrots, Brother Basil
in the corn, his beard a crimson cry
above the hue of the marrow. The bells
ring for matins, mid-day praise
and vespers, interrupting the drone
of drunken bees in the clover,
the circular rising through the air
of prayer. There is no answer without
a question, no excommunication
without a sin. Study and prayer, prayer
and study, the exquisite contemplation
of the butterfly's flight, the turning
of the worm. Beneath the modesty
of their robes, the knees
of Brothers Andrew and John
are scabbed; Basil will not bend.

His eye

His eye was on the sparrow
so he didn't see your heart
breaking, the man pushing
the old woman into the path
of the indifferent bus, the tooth
of the tiger shark glistening,
glistening, nor the trail of blood
it follows, didn't see
the pulse of flame on the horizon,
didn't hear the dull roar
of distant cannon. God isn't
dead, he is in a darkened room,
rubbing his eyes.

Religion and trouble

So far, all he'd had was religion
and trouble. The former kept him
going through the latter, which
always began at the end of the trail,
blue smoke clear through Tuesday.
Whiskey, women and bad habits
didn't faze him, he kept his mind
on the religion, its surety and promise
of better things yet to come, he
remembered the saints and martyrs
who'd risked the same temptations
and came through unscathed,
their reputations, at least. But
some days the trouble took hold
of him like weeds around the legs
of a swimmer and religion thinned
into smears of opaque cloud
above the horizon. Religion requires
faith, trouble has its way, believe it
or not.

.

Babel

Religion is the language
the snake employed when he
whispered to Eve, telling her
delicious lies. Reason is the language
God thundered to show his pique
that the snake had anticipated
his next move. Adam resisted
cynicism, a language whose time
had not yet come.

The naming

Bless the children, bless
their names, their faces,
their tongues, bless their hunger
which knows no want, bless the cries
they hurl out against
the indifference of the sky,
bless their silence, bless their sleep.

Bless their parents,
the bewildered older brothers,
the famished sisters, the aunts
who do their best with envy,
bless the grandparents who see the face
of death in the toothless smile
and are at peace, bless the woman
next door who will drop by, the girl
down the street who will learn
at this new altar. Bless the teachers,
the rabbi with dark hands, the red-faced priest
whose hands tremble, the scoutmaster
and his whistle, the butcher
in his apron, the man who drives
the ice cream truck with the bell, bless
the coach. Yes, bless the coach, who
will lovingly place the ball
in our hands, teach us the rules. Bless
the professors, the bureaucrats, the man
with the shriveled leg who sweeps,
the physician with his optimism, the lawyer
with his equivocation, the laundress, the maitre d'
in his ill-fitting tuxedo, his supercilious air.
Bless the supercilious air.
Bless the air.

And bless the bicycle, the sleek oil
of its chain, bless the bat, the glove,
the deck of cards, the book, yes,
by all means bless the book, let its pages
turn, let them turn us. Bless the high-rise,
the tenement, the house on the corner
with the green shutters and the flowers,
and bless the flowers, their seducing scent,
the bees, the honey they produce
against want. Bless the candle,
the night, the wind. Bless the stars that fill
the awesome sky and yes, bless
even the sky, that coldness, that heat.

Bless the goodness in us, the evil
lurking at the corner, trying to get in.
Bless the intentions, the good ones
and the ones not fully thought out,
the slip of the tongue, the turning
away. Yes, yes, bless the turning away,
even that, even that.

And come again then
to the children, to their names,
the sound of their names in our mouths,
to the reflection of the children in the clouds,
to the blessings they can expect,
all the blessings they are owed.

Jesus at ten

My father is a carpenter, a simple man,
my mother a good woman with a clear idea
of who she is, but there is something unsaid
between them, something unfinished.

A boy I know, a little older, John is his name,
can see the future, he does it for a *shekel*. He says
I'll have joys and sorrow, as many doubters
as followers, have sacrifices to make.

I tell this to my father who pauses at his bench,
his mouth bristling with nails of his own design.
He nods his head, says nothing. I have the feeling
sacrifice is something he knows of.

God shrugged

On the last day, God paused to consider
what he'd done. There'd been mistakes
but inspiration, ingenuity. He hadn't done
anything actually, merely allowed his thoughts
to take shape. Now he pondered the consequences,
good and evil, of course, but also beauty
and banality, ecstasy and pain. He saw
with exquisite clarity his error
and his genius, mirror images
of each other, the droplet of pure water
and the speck of dust caught
in an intricate balance that pleased
the esthete in him. He shrugged
and turned his mind to the creation
of religion.

Cain & Abel

Abel and Cain were bro's
with big plans for growing up,
meeting a pair of chicks
and double-dating at the Big Apple,
this drive-in outside town, then starting
a business of some sort, Adam and Sons
the sign would say except that Adam
had no head for business, he was
into sheep and that's all. Eve was partial
to Cain, her baby, but Adam favoured
his first-born, big Abel, and this pissed
Cain off something awful. *Suck the big one*,
Cain tells Abel, giving him a shove. *Oh yeah?*
Eat this, Abel says back and they're
at it, hormones rampant, blood high. Then Abel
does something dirty, *Mama's boy*, he calls
Cain and they both know she's the one
got them kicked out of the condo, her drinking
and tarting around. Cain winds up and delivers
a roundhouse right that would stun a horse
and Abel's no horse, he goes down like a sack
of cement. God says it was a suckerpunch
and scares Cain off the projects but I was there,
man, saw the whole thing, and the fight was
fair, that was a righteous punch
but a hell of a one all right. Cain, he
hightailed it for the territories, didn't
look back, didn't come back. So you kids
smarten up and play nice. Amen to that.

Triumph of the light

*— St. Peter's Cathedral, Muenster, Sask., decorated
with 80 life-sized figures and dozens of smaller
paintings by Berthold Imhoff (1868-1939)*

When Imhoff saw God what he saw was
light, circles of luminescence around the heads
of monks standing in as humble models
for even more pious men, an incandescent triangle
around the head of his vision of God
Himself, for whom no model dared sit, not even
Abbot Bruno, whose German profile inspired
the Roman nose of St. Paul.
                                        Imhoff took
a final look at the deep Saskatchewan sky and set
to work, his eyes closed the way he imagined
Michelangelo working, on his back, sweat
obscuring his vision. Paint flew from his brush
with divine direction, the faces and hands
of saints and angels taking shape without effort
or design. All of this is recorded
in his journal, the count's handwriting elegant
but cramped, his German unaffected by the years
in America, Canada, so far from the home
that oppressed him. *Feb. 26, 1921: today, the image
of Jesus that has eluded me revealed itself,
a stigmata in my hands. March 16: the darkness
overwhelms me. April 9: The lamb calls out
to me, praise to the lamb. May 4: I am blind,
the brilliance has won. June 12: Today we
finished, cleaned our brushes, stood back; tonight
word came that Bruno has died. God turns in ways
we cannot understand.*
                                        What is left
is the light, infusing the thinning paint as if the walls
were eggshell, onionskin, tears, the sky pulsing
with aurora borealis, the ceiling not a depiction
of heaven but heaven itself, heaven on earth, earth
filling itself up
with light.

The nuns' story

Years later, when they were old, the nuns
who'd lived in St. Scholastica remembered
most that they'd been cold. They paused
and smiled, sipping at their tea. It really
was a wonderful place, a wonderful life,
they said, the modesty of their Husband,
the splendor of His coat, the fragility
of their belief, like eggshells too sudden
to be taken for granted. They remembered
the way Brother Gerald flirted with them,
the students with faces open as handkerchiefs
fresh from the clothesline, the soft rise
and fall of their bosoms. In the summer there was
fresh beans and ice cream, in the winter
squash and coconut pudding, three varieties
of bread, always plenty. Their knees grew sore
in the garden, their necks chafed
under the wimple, the mattresses were narrow
and hard, the love they felt fierce and abrupt,
opening up like violet petals, the garden
their pride. But there was just one thing,
they said, pausing to reflect. In the abbey
where the brothers lived the radiators
crackled and hissed; in the convent
it was cold.

The Northern Lights disappoint

After two weeks keeping us
in the dark, the northern lights
arrive on the next to last night,
showing off like any kid, doing
backflips across the sky, a lot
of noise but not so much heat.
We keep peering up, hoping to see
God's face revealed behind the rent
in the sky, but he may be watching
the show someplace else, his neck
as sore as ours.

The order of things

The tree with its branches, the branches
and their nest, hidden in the leaves. The nest
with its bird, singing. The avuncular bird
with its worm. And the worm, what
of the worm? It sees the world
from an entirely different point
of view. It protests its innocence,
the benignness of its own nature,
the small but significant contribution
it plays in aeration of the soil. It cries
out against inequity, unfairness, rails
against the sinister plot that casts
it, the lowly worm, as some harbinger
of doom. Finally, it curses
the bird, wishing it indigestion
and worse. Does the bird care? No.
It eats the worm and sings all the louder.

Bad men who love Jesus

Bad men who love Jesus say his name
aloud in crowded rooms and to themselves
in the kitchen, they see his face in the cereal
bowl and on the blurred wings of blackbirds, that
sudden flash of red. They wash their hands
of him and imagine what must have been his pain
in the calluses of their palms, scratch their ankles
and think indulgently of his. Bad men who love Jesus
toast him with beer at the bar and fuck like Christ
in the back of their cars with the Magdalenes
from 20th Street. They cross his name off
calendar squares, take his name in vain while they
themselves are vain in his name, whistling with
admiration when they see themselves coming
up the street, so jaunty in their cocked hats
and polished boots. Bad men who love Jesus
hork and spit but don't think of themselves as bad
just as Jesus didn't think of himself as a christ, just
a carpenter's son with a gift for miracles
and pithy sayings. Only at the end did he lift
his eyes and think of his father, of how bad
he had been, all those nights in the desert, all
those temptations he had opened himself up
to, the spoiled fish and the multitudes and the Judas
kiss. "Forgive them," he asked his father, then
corrected himself. In his pain it had come to him
it was himself he sought forgiveness for.

Balm in Gilead

There is balm in Gilead
but until we reach there
we must suffer, that is the course
the father we never knew
set for us, so bitter was he
over the way we turned
on him. My love, yes, he
said, but earn it, earn it, earn
mine with your own. Then he
turned away, covering his ears,
went to Gilead to wait.

Adam's plan

While Eve was away, getting into what
would prove to be trouble, Adam was pacing
off the dimensions of the orchard, turning
his mind to the intricacies of a fence, what
to leave in, what to put out, the best location
for a gate. That it never came to be is
an accident of history, and it would be
generations before the idea of a fence arose
again, but by that time the orchard had fallen
into disuse, the trunks and limbs of the plum
and peach twisted, the fragrant fruit rotting
on the mossy floor of the tangled forest that
had grown up around it where exposed roots
lay in wait for ankles that never strayed
that way, fence or not, the dimensions now
impossible to calculate, Adam's plan
impossible to decipher.

Where Jesus went
(for Art Slade)

I been everywhere that Jesus went
and I didn't see him anywhere. Egypt,
1917, we fought from the Dead Sea
to the Red Sea, Suez, up and down
that damn Sinai from Palestine to Sunday
and back. Ate sand for breakfast, lunch
and supper and sometimes that was all
we ate. Water, we got a gallon a day
a man, share with your horse, up to you
how you divvy it up but if the horse
dies you're as good as dead. Saw men
dead, dying, wishing they were dead, wishing
they'd never been born, saw bullet wounds,
knife wounds, men who stepped on mines
where all that was left was more wound
than man. Heard howling at the moon,
heard prayer, heard the night fill up
with a silence big as religion, saw the moon
on fire, the sun iced over. Up and down
that damn desert, Holy Land they
call it. Never saw one damn sign
of God.

Noah's complaint

The sound of rain
bleating down with cries
of pain and dread, nubby sheets
of rain falling with grace
on the parched hearts
of the departed, eyelashes
of rain fluttering onto cheeks
already damp with tears, bellyaches
of rain protesting too much, acres
of rain, fists of rain, an open hand
filled to the brim with rain, a longing
in the gut, a crying out for rain, a dream
of rain that never came, a shaking
of the head against the rain, a lowering
of the head, acquiescence, a prayer, a kiss,
a promise.

Another view of the garden

When God saw what Eve did he
just lost it, shook his head the way
any disappointed father would, the thought
of the snake's soft tongue on her paperwhite skin
turning his heavenly scrotum tight and round
as a peach, and he threw a fit, drove her
and poor blameless Adam away
from the darkened door, turned his own back
on the whole sorry mess and went for a sulking walk
by the river, the air above his cold shoulders
fomenting heavy weather. Since then he's lost
interest, as likely to be grouchy as glad, but that's
the way it is, isn't it, with children, not ungrateful
but their heads filled with their own sense
of themselves, not what we might dream them
to be. And as for Eve, she dreamed of sons.

The photographer's eye
(St. Peter's Abbey, Muenster, Sask.)

To the photographer's eye there are
few certainties, the only blacks
in the monks' cassocks, the only whites
a bleached sky, all else infinite shades of grey
and shadow. The verdant abbey garden struck
dumb in its bath of grey as if transmogrified
to fungus, graceful limbs of trees suspended
in time as they are in space. Only the artifacts
spring to life, the chalice and aspergillum breathing
in artificial light. His is an overcast world, as free
of moral compass as it is of sun, of colour,
the sensual curve of Brother Michael's leg
a temptation, Brother Anthony's glance
off the frame an alluring diversion. Follow
me, Anthony seems to be saying, the print
bleeding out of itself as if to suggest
the impossible possibility.

Sparrows

But not His eye, His heart.
That beating of wings is His own breath,
that eruption of feather, beak and talon
His exhalation, every ragged lift into air
from pond and meadow the rising
of His chest, every settling, the fall. If
Thoreau and Emerson were right, then
the trembling limb is Holy Spirit, all
that we need. The song
of the meadowlark, heaven.

Original sin

"Comfort me with apples, for I am sick of love
"Refresh me with apples, for I am faint with love"
- The Song of Solomon

The truth about Adam and Eve
is not that she ate of the apple or that her husband
was seduced into sin, but that over the years
some of the sweetness between them soured,
like wine going to vinegar, and they didn't know it.
Original sin was not their arrogance but
stupidity, blindness. There came a day
when the taste in Eve's mouth was too bitter
for her to accept and she looked at Adam
with new eyes, eyes clouded over by a patina
of years. Adam, for his part, was restless,
dissatisfied, but he didn't know its source,
couldn't guess at its remedy. They blamed
each other for what had become of their children,
the dissolution of the garden, the anarchy
of the animals. Adam cast about and couldn't bring
himself to admit he loved her any less. Instead, he
blamed the apple, just barely remembered. And Eve,
as unwilling as he to acknowledge the weakness, cast
her curse on the guileless snake. And the sin,
if there ever really was one, multiplied. They were
cast out, not from the garden, but from the holiness
of their love. It hurt God to see them this way.
Perhaps *that* was the sin.

After the rain

After the rain the sun comes out
in its brightest Florida shirt, flashing
its teeth and showing its tan
to impress the girls. You feel like a child
again, the air all lemony
and the light slippery as soapsuds
in the bath. Across the lake, the trees
stand up one at a time, soldiers
at inspection, the acid smell of moss
rising in the electric air all the way
to heaven, its windows
thrown open. God's wife sweeps
the walk, shakes out the pillows,
braids her hair in the sunshine
before going in to make beds
tousled through the long night
of rain, the turning away. It pleases
her to see her man back at work.

Theology

A quarter moon hangs low in the morning sky,
a thumbprint reminder that night is not through
with us, oh no, not yet. Day, night, light, dark,
the cycle carries on with tedious regularity, each
extreme laying a trail of clues leading inextricably
to the other. The seasons too pass in their cycle,
and the ages, infancy to infirmity and through
the transmigration of souls into infancy again
if that's what you care to believe. The tides rise
and fall, the leaf buds, greens, browns, withers
all according to plan. And where is God in all
this? Puppetmaster, enmeshed in his own strings,
or tourist, folding and refolding a map? The creases
are worn thin from this incessant folding, creating
the illusion of unintended routes, a false cartography.
Like any man, God is reluctant to ask directions.
He batters on, against his own idea of tide,
seeking a way.

The hangover

Friday night and the sky opens, God peers
down with a frown, an unexpected eclipse.
What's become of the covenant to honour
the sabbath? There they go, their mouths
filled with golden teeth and hunger, eyes glazed
over from a light of their own making. They
sing, they dance, they let their heads
explode with possibility, but what
of the promise, the solemn dusting of knees
on the hardwood floor, the keeping
of lists? The sound of a car door rusting
against a curb, the milkman's jingle, the thirst
that catches at your throat before sleep, you know
there's a reckoning, something even worse
than the hangover. You look up, pray for rain.

A blessing on the day
(for the September dead)

The dawn prays itself out of holy night, wills
itself into holy day, clouds bowing their heads
to the holy presence of light. All light
is holy, all darkness, the full and the empty
of horizons. The land is holy, the sea, air
is holy, the humours of the body, blood
and phlegm, bile and black bile, the purity
of the spirit, the echo of a lie. The paradox
of life which ends with death is holy, the comfort
of death which crowns life is holy, the irony
of laughter, the cruelty of a smile, the glistening
of teeth beneath the innocent lip, all these are holy,
the orchestration of songbirds, the black dirge
of crows, all holy, the worm in the beak
of the bird in the nest of the flowering tree,
its scent rising all the way to heaven, holy heaven.
All certainties are holy, all promises, all doubts.
A traffic light is holy, the green, the yellow,
the red, the hum and rattle of traffic, the dust
it raises, the receding red light of the taillamp
in the falling dusk. And night, holy night, praying
its way out of the ashes of holy day.

Arts and Letters

The weather

In the night the weather
turned, temperature falling
like the shooting stars
we stayed up late to watch,
our necks stiff, throats hot
with gin and Drambuie. In our bunks
later, we shivered with delight
and cold, raiding the cupboards
for blankets, turning ourselves
into burrowed mice beneath
the hoary pile. We scratched poems
in the window frost
capturing the beauty
of it all but just before dawn
the power surged and we awake
to blank screens,
their memories as faulty as ours.

Another creation myth
(for June McClintick)

The painting takes shape
like cloud unrolling itself
across the horizon, absorbing
sky into its concentration,
its multiplicity. Fuchsias appear
in the upper left, rich, sexual bulbs
pungent with the aroma that drives bees
into frenzy, stamen and stigma
erect, quivering in anaemic air.
A wash of blue streaks across the centre
of the canvas, dark fading to light,
and the faint outline of an imperfect moon
pulses below the flowers, a smudge
of dark suggesting a bird superimposed.
The next day, the smudge has cocooned itself
into a hummingbird, its juvenile throat
and eye determined but dull, and by evening
a stand of birch has begun to emerge
from the undeveloped field lower right, each tree
a tooth in the canvas's grinning mouth. The moon
waxes and wanes, clouds over, shines
through again, casting its brilliant smile
over the hummingbird's metallic throat, its fierce
eye. The earth beneath the trees grows rich
and moist with humus, lichen and moss, tangled
with roots, the grin broadening, teeth reflecting
the moon's immodest blush. The sky glows. Too much
so, perhaps. The painter steps back, steps
forward, raises her brush. Once again, she
is god, and this still
only the fifth day.

Reading poems at McIntosh Point
(for Jacquie Bell)

Reading poems by flashlight at McIntosh Point,
I can see the way the sense behind the sense
of the words takes shape, riding up the trail
of moths to the almost-perfect moon,
its missing smudge shedding light
on what's missing in the poems. We sit
huddled around three tables
on a patio lit by Christmas strings
and the critical moon, a group of friends
with beer, the work we've produced
over the last few days, a flashlight
to illuminate what might not otherwise
be apparent. Someone laughs, we murmur
in the appropriate places, the writers
pleased as grandmothers trotting out
photos of children at play. The words
strike the ear with the clicking certainty
of a typewriter key, that much amazement
at their own existence, that much finality.
You read a poem that moves within me
like the eyes of the bear we saw from the car
driving here, the frightened menace, the awe.
The beer is cold as the night, and I shiver.

Little mysteries

The woman with the Boston accent
is trying hard not to say anything
but the vowels she fears are conspiring
to unfoot her send her sprawling
in the paint-spattered street. What could she say
that would be so bad in this crowd
where the K's bash up against the M's
like cousins from the same village
out on the dance floor with nothing
but left feet between them? The fiddler
takes his cue from the smiling sailor
at the door, wiping his hands on the apron
of the baker's wife, a fine dusting
of flour *poof*ing into the air above
their heads like spores from a mushroom
deep within the azure forest, beyond the dam
of the agreeable beavers, their teeth
so much more benign than she had imagined.
She observes all this, commits it
to memory, her fingers assuming the shape
of stripped twigs. All is mystery, a puzzle
like the shaving of spiralling rusted metal
she found in deer-flattened grass
just before the place where the bear
proves his worth, giving the seeds
of berries back to the earth. For years,
she has collected objects
to paint, now she finds the objects
have a pull of their own, their own formula,
another of life's little mysteries.
The iron corkscrew points to the north
or the south, depending on how you hold
it, the air which surrounds it filling
itself up with a special light, a light
through which, squinting, even she can see.

Afternoon rain

Midafternoon the sky changes
its mind, rain galloping down
on a dead run, the computer screen
flickers and I hesitate a moment
before saving what I've been working
on but then the power doesn't go
out and I have no excuse
but to carry on, the words pulling
me through the weather's lie, past
the tea cooling in its cup, the cigarette
I can only imagine, the words moving
me along the rhythm of my own breathing,
the scattering gravel of rain
on the tar roof, the words spelling
out their own logic, their own reason,
marking out the limits
of their season. The cursor's pulse
is my own, the filling page my heart
filling with liquor distilled
by my tongue, the beating on the roof
a music I compose for you. The rain ends
with a sigh, the sky wincing,
the screen flickers, the poem
shines in the new light.

Dylan in Duluth

After the lights go out and he's standing
behind the curtain listening to the freight-train roar
of applause, waiting to go out one last time,
he gets this whiff of sweat and piss over
the incense, another drafty hockey rink and this one
too damn close to home, and he gets to thinking
of someone - who do you suppose it might be,
Woody, maybe, old Woody and Cisco and
rambling Jack, Little Arlo maybe, or Joannie,
Joannie and Joni, maybe, or Koop and some
of the old gang he used to hang with back
in the old days in the Village - but, no, it's
the Big Bopper, Chantilly lace and a pretty face,
yeah, the old Big Bop himself, dead all these years,
bit the big one along with Holly and Ritchie Whatshisname
in a farmer's field just down the road
a ways, that road at the edge of town he'd noticed
near the airport, heading south and forever, just like
at home, all gravel and heatwaves.

                                        That plane
must have really smelled of sweat and piss
in its last moments, Holly and Whatshisname
singing out a clear harmony of fright, but he imagined
the Bop was silent, stoic in the dizzying face
of his fate, either that or too blind drunk to know. Oh,
Baby. He thinks of all the planes he's been on,
all the close calls, thinks about all the lies
he's told, all the truths he's hinted at, stumbled
toward. They made a cult of Holly, scissored his likeness
out of the clear night sky and pasted it onto fridges
long past their due date, and the other guy, Ritchie, he
was another one spared the indignity of growing old
with everyone watching, forever young
in the broken corn, ribbons and bows, ribbons
and bows. But it was the Bop he'd always
liked, admired, oh, a no-talent clown, sure, but the man
had style, and he knew something most of us take
a lifetime of rock and roll to figure out. That's what
it's really all about, isn't it, a face, burning
in the third row, a face you can't ever forget, a face
caught in your throat, a scrap of lace.

Pentimento
(for Christine Lynne)

Going to the bar was the mistake
Christine has to live with the next day,
not just the lost time but
her perspective out of whack,
ladling on the paint by the bucketful
all in aid of lightness but producing
just the opposite. The reeds she wants
so badly to dance grow heavy-thighed,
lead-footed, start to sink
into the marsh, decaying like Lindner's
rotted trunks rather than breathing,
the way she can feel them. The more
she pushes the paint in one direction,
the more it pushes back in the other
until finally the canvas itself seems
to be sinking under its own weight. What
to do? At dinner, she growls, beats
her chest, grumbles about the bar, the poolgame,
the way the jukebox blared its way
into her dreams, the headache that extended
all the way through her arms
to her fingers, the brushes, the points
of light gone out of control. The woman
in the next studio sticks her head
around the partition, there's a smear
of green paint on her nose gives her
a comical look, as if nothing it sniffs at
could ever smell too bad. "Had a bad day,
eh?" she says cheerfully. Yes, Christine
agrees, a bad day, but paint has a way
of finding its own balance, of springing
back under weight the way reeds bent down
resume their posture, their roots
blindly seeking water, shoots rising
toward sun, and always, despite
the weather, finding the dance.

Fire or ice

(for David Carpenter)

The night of the day W.O. kicks, Carp gets
philosophical, thinking out loud about
a young friend whose novel stopped dead
in its tracks when he stumbled into love,
worried that a man who can't write
through love maybe isn't really a writer
after all. Earlier, he'd been telling a story
about how when he was a grad student
W.O. told him one day that he planned to write
five more novels, old man or not, and sketched
them out. "Damned if he didn't write them
all," Carp said, but the conjunction of an old man
dying and a young man slipping into silence
sends a shiver up Carp's spine, makes him
remember the frozen stick he'd been once
himself, his head a lump of ice, his heart
a no-man's land, an arctic circle
burning with stay-away warnings through
his chest. He thinks about the woman who melted
all that ice, the way her touch set him on fire, goosing
the writer in *him*, and he worries now about what
may be ahead, fire or ice. He remembers
too the cabin he lived in back then, the frost
on the windows, and the house in town he'd go to
when he was bushed, a house filled with dancers,
the lovely arched necks of the women, the feet
that never touched the floor.

Croc

Poets could learn a lot from crocodiles,
the way they hinge their mouths open,
the sharpness of their teeth, the way
they invite birds in to clean their teeth,
serving up banquets of dead meat,
the eloquence of their tears.

Our mouths are stumble-tongued
with metaphor, scraps of images
from old poems stinking up our efforts
at new ones, crying out for the prying beaks
of critical birds.

Romance

Jane Austen said the world
was round, that sooner or later
a maid adrift in such a world
would encounter a rounder, that love
was not only certain but certain
to go bad but then, as the world
turned, turn good again. This was
the optimism of her age. The Brontes
all agreed. Brian Wilson said
the world was flat, that love grew
on its underside, that the only way
to reach it was tunneling, looking
down to see the light. Oh yeah,
sing the backup girls, oh yeah,
oh yeah.

The visiting writer

The girl in the front row wants
to know where you get your ideas,
why the story ends where it does,
the significance of the phone call,
and thank goodness at least she doesn't
ask about theme. The questions
keep tumbling out of her and you start
to wonder if she's the class brain or
a compulsive mouth, but the other kids
don't seem to mind, don't even seem
to notice, really, as if she has her role,
this is it, and they have theirs, sitting
back and listening, and what,
you start to wonder, is yours? Well, you're
being paid, thank God, and so's the teacher,
who's playing Buddha and enjoying it all,
the things you say are no skin off his ass,
after all, and the kids are the original
captive audience, some of them even look
interested, not just amused and distracted,
and one or two, the girl who can't shut up
and a boy who gazes at you
with such dark-eyed intensity
you start to feel uncomfortable, may dream
about you tonight, may carry a splinter
of something you say with them
all their lives, and some of them, a different girl,
another boy altogether, may dine out for years
on the tale of how Laura strung out
the visiting writer until the bell rang, really
had him going.

Portrait of the artist doing laundry
(for Betsy Rosenwald)

Betsy moves Chris's load to the dryer
and sets in folding her own while her mind
wanders, registering the pattern
of the steam pipes, the texture
of the stippled walls. The faded colours
of her undies, their patterns
and shapes, continue to amaze
her, giving as much pleasure now
as when they were bright. She thinks
about the sticks she gathered in the woods
this morning, the heft of them, the feel
of the rough bark in her palm, the smooth
pale pith beneath, tender as the flesh
of her own thigh. She considers
the structure she will make
of them, the way the pieces
will come together. In her hands
the collar of her flannel shirt
is still warm, nubbed, like the skin
of a lover in the cave of their bed. She
folds and refolds the shirt, just so.

Living in a cartoon world

Above his peaceful face, a cartoon log
is being sawed in half. He opens
his eyes and a cartoon lightbulb goes
on, signaling inspiration. He doesn't see
the banana peel and when he leaps to his feet
he bangs against the exclamation mark, shattering
the bulb. A string of punctuation marks
and printers' symbols fly from his mouth
and his eyes roll back, revealing
the whites. Stars and comets swirl
around his head and a yellow canary
whistles as he arcs gracefully to the ground
with a *thud*. Within a frame, there are Xs
where his eyes were and he doesn't hear
the banging at the door, can't see
it's a tweety bird. Real life
is hard enough; trying to lighten up
can be deadly.

The poem unawares

How to write the poem
without being aware
of the poem? How to think
without thinking, to escape
the thought? How to tell you
I love you without having to see
the way your eyes flick away, the set
of your perfect mouth? How to fly
without wings, how to say
words in a language you
cannot know? How to know
the unknowable? How to look
into God's eye without blinking, how
to close the door that isn't open, to catch
the breath that refuses to be caught? How
to not be so damned
self-conscious.

Victor's children

The hunchback of Notre Dame
and Jean Val Jean meet in the afterlife
to compare Broadway notes. They sit
in a drafty café in the third department
of Heaven, dunking day-old crusty bread
into large bowls of *café latte*. The Phantom
is conspicuously absent but, as Val Jean
remarks, "he's not really one of us."
The hunchback agrees. "A different sort
altogether." They give thanks
to the Creator but most of all to
their creator and the producers
and the actors who had infused them
with the most life. "It's hard to be played
by a hack," muses the hunchback, who
has heard his lines mangled
in a hundred knockoff shows.
Hugo, they agree, was a genius, though
the hunchback complains of some
of the master's youthful excess, and Jean
believes that the darker shades
of his personality are the product
of a creeping cynicism that coloured
the great romantic's old age. But never mind,
genius will out, and they wave to the *garçon*
for second cups. After a silence, broken
only by the clinking of spoons on china,
Val Jean puts his hand on the tattered sleeve
of the hunchback. "Did you suffer much?"
he inquires, glancing away. The hunchback
merely shrugs. "It was bearable. And you?"
Val Jean takes a long time before he replies.
"It was for art," he says. "Yes," agrees
the hunchback. "For art."

Phases of the Moon

Moonshine

The moon's idea of a good time
is to rise and shine, casting
its brilliant smile in the path
of some bright fellow with an idea
of his own. He gazes up, getting
a crook in his neck, and lets
his mind take the path of least
insistence, waxing poetic
over the charms of a charmer who
also has ideas, the obvious rhymes
cast aside for something more
to the liking of the object
of his desire. The moon sees
all this and is pleased, setting
its sights on the sizzling sink
into the horizon, its glimmer path
leading the way for all the lovers
who've been hanging on, their strength
waning as the night thins. The sated moon
knows it *also* rises, that tomorrow
brings another night,
and another.

Last words

There were no last words,
both the dying and the death
left him speechless. Afterwards,
though, his handwriting laid siege,
ambushing us from the pages
of books, the backs of photos, margins
of the documents he left behind
to be dealt with. His hand-written will
filled our eyes with his presence,
the slanted sprawl, illegible
in tangles, falling in on itself,
studded with words like "darling"
and "beloved." The suits of clothes
in the basement spoke to us too,
the threadbare shirts, ties asking
to be straightened, a hat adrift
without its jaunty angle. All around us,
reminders
of what we needn't be reminded of,
whispers
in the dark.

x

Dem bells

The dinner bell rings
at noon, its cheerful clamour
a call to the hunger
of the ear, the desire
of the ear to be filled
with a sound pure and hearty
as soup, salad, sandwich.

The wedding bell sounds
midafternoon, filling the sky
with promises and promise,
premise and premises, rice
cascading from the curled hands
of the inlaws, their throats
gone sore with shouting.

Finally the funeral bell
weighs in, silencing
its colleagues with the weight
of its sonorous tones, the implication
of its echo. Its ringing
takes the breath right out
of us, leaves us without voice,

without ears.

A small hotel

Through the trees and past the swings
to the baseball diamond, then you'll see
the lake on your left. Down that path
there was a hotel by the edge of the water
but they moved it, oh years ago. They say
the ghosts of the guests still dwell there
where their rooms were, endlessly calling
room service. In the darkest nights you
can hear one in particular, an old man
who would meet his darling every summer
just for a few afternoons, a handful of plums
to be eaten from the hand. You can hear
his voice calling her name over the pounding
of the waves and the raucous of the ravens,
that's what they say. Him calling her, the silence
of her reply.

In love with decay

I stood in line at the Safeway, my basket laden
with rotting fruit, cherries glutinous
in their sugared blood, blueberries marbled
with sepulchral mould, molten strawberries
laced with slime and fragrant as sulfur, peaches
and plums all softboiled eggs, all puppy belly.

A woman in a flowered dress and cheeks rosy
as a newborn's turned away, holding
her nose, but the checkout clerk looked through
me, saw that I was in love with decay, with the rapture
of destruction. Gently, she placed my purchases
in a paper bag she drew from under the till,
jewels too precious for plastic. Then I set off
home, drunk with the possibilities of life.

What was it Eliot said?

The hair in my nostrils grows white. My penis
stretches, yawns, rolls over into its pillow, desire
courses through me like flickering light
in a storm. A mosquito bows its head at the well
of my pale blood and hesitates. My joints
sing, *a cappella,* empty palms ache. Outside
the window, sparrows congregate at the feeder
like old women on the stoops of Brooklyn
when I was a boy, noisy and vivid in their scarves,
arms filled with the absence of their children, lost
in the war or to illnesses now mercifully extinct.
These birds regard me as the women might,
with neither contempt nor indifference, they know
I feed them, asking nothing in return,
and their gratitude pulses in the blue sheen
of their throats, but remains unspoken. When I open
the door, they explode like gravel sprayed
from the tires of a speeding car. Their song
thrums in the absence their shape carves
into the fragrant air, a reproach, a warning.

Unexpected

Under the shutters, bats cling
in the dark to what they know
to be true, the way you and I hold
on to the sense we have
of everything unfolding
just the way it should. This is the way
things are supposed to be, the way
the mind that dreamt us
imagined, what was hoped. What
wasn't expected was the dark.

The bears

All week they shadow us, keeping out
of reach, almost out of sight, piles
of their leavings on the trail where
they can't be missed, berry bushes
stripped and flattened, their hoarse laughter
around the bend of the trail. We hear reports
of them at Murray Point, a sow
and three cubs tangled in clotheslines, and sighs
in the dark as we hurry to the showers
in our brave nightshirts, shadows rippling
on ahead, the peopled woods lovely
and deep. One evening from the car we see
a dark young stranger, ambling
across the road, bright eyes dumbfounded
by the UFO crossing his path, eager to get
home with his stories. Yesterday, the trashcans
lining the cottage road outside the camp gates
are knocked over, garbage strewn, someone
sees the cubs meandering through, strips
of yellow plastic bags trailing
from their anxious jaws. Still, we go
for our evening walk, spooked but braced
somehow by their presence, whatever spirit
moves them moving among us, giving us
fool's courage. It is the encounter we dread
that we long for, that moment when our eyes
might meet theirs, catch a glimpse
of the wildness they carry within them,
that we abandoned.

So it is a blow, knocking
the wind out of us, wind and something else,
when we hear today they've been shot, our family
of four and another youngster, the teenager
we saw from the car probably, and trackers
are closing in on another at the point.
They don't bother with tranquillizers
anymore, too dangerous, there's too many
anyway, and once they're weaned to garbage
they're spoiled – we listen to all this
in stunned silence, lips moving slowly
the way our handsome loner on the road moved
with dark startled grace. "They didn't have to
do that," Betsy whispers. Later, we find
blood and rifle casings on the road, like refuse
from the overturned cans. Brenda sprinkles
tobacco, chants a prayer, our steps
move heavily across elastic moss, the woods
silent and empty today. The woods empty.

West to east

We went from west to east or east
to west, that wasn't important, what was
important was the direction we arrived
at, not the point we'd come from
but the vision our eyes held before
us, not milk and honey but bread
and water, water deep and cold enough
to make our teeth ache, black bread
to make the tongue ache, still warm
from the oven, its crust protesting
in our hands, the hypodermic smell
of caraway and yeast vivid in our nostrils.

We went from west to east and arrived
at a conclusion we couldn't have foreseen,
went from east to west following a sun
that hasn't yet set.

Worm's eye view

A world, spinning through clouds
insubstantial as your breath
on a morning in January.
On the world, puddles of cobalt, islands
of emerald, cinnamon, ivory.
On this island, hills, mountains,
forests, plains, meadows.
At the edge of this meadow, a tree,
American elm, gritting its teeth
against the remorseless stare
of the beetle, its arms raised
in resignation. In the crook
of one branch, a nest, a whorl
of grass, earth, twigs, a frightwig.
In the nest, a bird, its breast
raging, its eye vivid. In the beak
of the bird, a worm, more resigned
than even the tree. In the eye
of the worm, a world, spinning
through insubstantial cloud.

The man in the moon

Tonight the moon is old cheddar,
not fey blue, you can almost taste
its bite, the man on the canapé
smirking to some private joke
at your expense, you can be sure.
What must he think of us! That
our rotation controls the tides
of his dead seas, brings colour
to the face of his beloved, drives
moondogs mad. In sanguine moods
he composes sonatas to our beauty,
makes wishes on us; feeling lusty,
he howls. We wane, his feelings
lag, we wax, he grows robust, we
set and tears bright as stars
from neighbouring constellations
roll down his chubby cheeks. A full Earth
inspires poetry.

The view west

Changing rooms in the middle
of the week, a misunderstanding,
I have occasion to stand for a moment
on the landing with a view west, the sun
a painful gulp in the throat of God, the river
a knot in his leg, throbbing. The desk clerk
is apologetic, the bellboy angling
for advantage but I am happy enough
to get another start. In the old room, the east
slunk outside my window like a fighter
living down his last performance, sparring
with his own shadows. From the new window
the sun gets a head start it could use
to put the bellman to shame, the same
grubby rooftops, the same brave line
of laundry, only its heartburned heartbeat tripping
a moment faster. Turning my head, I can't help
but remember the view west, the slow ache.

The virtue of snow

Freezing rain turning to sleet, winds
gusting to 40 kph, temperatures dropping
to -20, windchill 1900
— weather forecast

Head down through needle snow,
all the resolve you had
to push on the certain distance
begins to waver – how can anything
melt in this cold, you wonder,

and so fast. The wind picks its way
through you like soldiers dancing
across minefields, careful but predatory,
and that sighing in the trees is the breath
of frozen beasts, their hearts rekindled

by your pain. A handful of fire
would be heaven, not hell, a bathtubful
pure bliss compared to the mortal heat
the hollow night is breathing down
your neck, giving your ear an unwanted kiss

and in the ditch, the comfort of snow
up to your knees, the virtue of sleep
calls your name in a voice you
can't possibly recognize, whispers
lies and truth and lies again until

you can't distinguish. The virtue
of vice is a paradox even weather
can't blur, blow those winds of February
though they do, blowing their icy hearts
out, mouth to mouth resuscitation.

The war

We came down from the mountains
and filled the valley, we filled the valley
with blood, your blood and our own good blood,
we gave a life for every one we took, we took
one for each one you had taken. Then we
retired to a grove of pecan trees by a brook
to take stock: we saw that our numbers
had shrunk and we grieved but we didn't
anger because we knew you had been
provoked; we recorded our victories and we
were jubilant. Then we gathered our injured
and our armour and began the long march
home, well satisfied.

The philosopher bear

The bear shits in the woods,
then the bear pauses to consider
the implications of his action.
He sits on a nearby stump
and wonders what people
walking by will think
when they come upon the stink.
He considers the effect
on the aquifer, the water table,
the delicate forest ecosystem,
air quality, tourism, downstream agriculture,
sustainable renewable development,
microeconomics and macrobiotics.
He ponders the moral dilemma,
the social ramifications,
the philosophical question,
the precarious balance of good
and evil, the meaning of life
and whether or not God still cares.
If a bear shits in the forest,
he wonders, and no one is there
to smell it, does it really stink?
The bear sits for a long time
reflecting on these questions. Spring
passes, then summer, the first leaves
of autumn fall on him and the night air
quickens. The blueberries
are long gone, and sleep calls. He thinks
of his cave, his favourite pillow,
the eiderdown comforter. *Ah, fuck it,*
he decides, *I'm only a bear.*

The dark

The flashlight is a shovel, carving a hole
in the dark I move through with safety,
the dark a terrier biting at my heels.
The headlights of a speeding car are augers
drilling tunnels in the dark through which
the sea crashes, the dark, terrible sea.
The stars are hornets stinging holes in the dark
to let the light of tomorrow shine, giving us hope.
The moon is a wound in the face of the dark,
its plans for us clear enough if you stand still,
if you look closely enough. The streetlamp
on the corner, the glowing windows of the house
at the end of the street are sirens, tempting
the dark to do something it will regret, but
the dark is staunch, unafraid. It rears back,
hissing.

Communion of the wasps

They came straight up, the wasps, not from above
as you might expect but from the ground, as if
the earth were releasing all the demons
as children we were told inhabit it. They swarmed
over us, as frantic as we were, we to escape, they
to spread their love, to prove it. Their need, they bore
on their sleeves, emblems of the venom they carry
not for harm but sacrament. Our need was deeper, the pain
hurrying us along the path, stripping our clothes
from us, ribbons of music erupting from our mouths
more in fright than pain, music that charted the course
of our need, of its hunger. The wasps circled,
conferred, looked into themselves for the strength
they needed for pursuit but fell short. Our need
was greater, for escape, for comfort, to look
into ourselves and see a reflection less like that
of the wasps, the fear etched on our eyes, the rancid
smell of it. They came to us as supplicants, seeking
communion, faith, offering sacrifice. We turned
our backs on them, aloof gods, their belief in us
not strong enough to sustain our own. They brought
us the only gift they knew, we spat it out.

The Beautiful Wives

Happy endings

The wolf was just there, ahead on the trail.
When she turned around, there was another one
behind. The first one was wrapping a belt
around its paw, a big thick Garrison
with studs. The second one had a shiv.
They both had evil grins on their snouts,
teeth glinting with spit. What to do,
with Grandmother's house still a mile
through the woods and even the birds hushed
now, darkness closing in? Wasn't there something
in the Grimm's Guide about this eventuality,
something that would allow a resourceful girl
to avoid the trap of waiting for Prince Charming
to save her, the crowing afterward, the rescue
as bad as the danger? She checked her map
but the happy ending she hoped for
wasn't marked and she'd have to find her way
herself. Just then, the first wolf stepped
closer, opened its rank mouth
and spoke.

Semi-tough

Your black leather jacket
swaggers its way out
of the closet, shouldering me
aside. Your motorcycle boots
with the silver toes give me a glimpse
of heel and your studded Garrison belt
curls itself around its own slim fist
with lip-licking menace. The stud
in your tongue
sticks itself out. Is it merely
the mirror that trembles?

Six two

(for Pien)

Six foot two gives a man
a certain perspective, Tom says,
laughing down at the breakfast table,
crumbs on his lips. They don't sleep
together anymore, not that way,
broke up after four years because it
didn't seem to be going anywhere,
irreconcilable differences, he mimes, but they're
still good pals, and once in a while he sleeps
over, a meal out together and a jog, then
chaste and snug as a pair of polished spoons
in her third kitchen drawer, the one
he keeps promising to fix. She still loves him
and it makes her glad, the thought
that this time might be different, and it
makes her cry when it isn't. She's
no shrimp, average height though lean
as a salmon, but he calls her
Shorty, likes to kid that she's just not up
to his standards, to the imaginary line
on the kitchen wall. Six two gives a man
not a right but a temptation.

The goose-plucker's daughter
(with apologies to David Carpenter and Richard Ford)

The goose-plucker's daughter was the one
whose hands actually dug into down, hands
that had other talents too, that's what the man
at the general store implied, his wife's eyebrows
pointing toward the rafters. She lived in a fifth wheel
parked next to an abandoned shed within sight
of the church where four generations of her kin
were buried, above the coulee. Now her brothers
were in jail not so much for killing a man
but for boasting about it, the family blood running
thin as water from the pipe beside the garage
where hunters could fill their jugs
for a quarter. Two bits for water, three bucks
each for the geese and a double sawbuck
for whatever else took place
in the fifth wheel, and the best damn goosemeat
in Saskatchewan thrown into the bargain, the long sky
all filled up with rain.

A man's world

The snowman greets the sun
with caution, with apprehension,
with resignation. The gingerbreadman
regards the oven with suspicion,
the appetites of children
with horror. The breadman
and the milkman are sanguine
about the ironies of life, a feeling
not shared by the mailman, for whom
bad news is stock and trade. The fireman
is hotheaded, the policeman partial
to arts martial and vivid, the boogieman
not what he seems, drawing his rhythm
from the stars. A woman
is a marvel, marvelous and marveling
at all she sees, while the clergyman
says a prayer for the snowman,
knowing that stoicism goes only
so far.

She leaves her husband

*Ms. Gwyn once wrote that the regret of her life was
that she never had children. She leaves her husband.*
                                    — news item

Mornings, sleep still in her eyes, she shakes
the pillow the way her grandmother shook
the dust from her skirt leaving that Polish town
she never regretted, would sometimes confess
to grandchildren not even remembering being born
in, so much had she made her future into a present,
even a past. He's still asleep and why couldn't she
do the same, forget she'd ever even had a life
with him, happy though it was at its beginnings, why
couldn't she start again as if for the first time,
her whole life still ahead of her. She foregoes
her shower and dresses quietly as she can,
the bright dress he liked so much once, the shoes
that never quite matched, and takes a few things
from her drawer and closet shelf, stuffing them
into a duffel bag in the next room. She'll have
coffee later, she'll have everything she can imagine
later, but now there is just the matter of the note,
the unforgettable good-bye. This is, she knows,
the moment that for years will define her, take
her pulse, the moment when she shakes her head
and steps carefully through the door
and into herself.

86

Desire

A woman collecting wildflowers
by the lake's edge, her eyes filled
with the anticipation that springs
from an innocence beyond the scope
of the heart. She is driven by no hunger
for food nor shelter, nor for sex
or companionship, she is worried
not one whit over her husband
and his eccentricities, her darling children
and their tattoos, the multitude
of their earrings, she seeks neither comfort
nor excitement. The flowers on their stalks
glow smugly, they are filled
only with themselves, the prospect
of the woman's vase holds no interest
for them, they will be content wherever
they are. For a moment, the arc
of her desire and theirs cross
and her hand trembles.

Stolen car report
(for Kathy Donovan)

Tumbling downstairs, sleep and sun in her eyes,
the first thing Kathy sees out the living room window
she scrubbed so hard last summer is an absence,
pure streetscape where the car should be, not even a puff
of exhaust or an oil stain to mark its passing.
The long tedium of the cops and the neighbours, nobody
seeing or hearing a thing, and then shanks mare to work,
not all that far thank God, and back again, the detour
to the grocery, out again in the evening for that reading
she wanted to catch, coffee with a friend, her legs
starting to ache from all that walking, more than she's
done in years, in the morning, she knows, they'll
really be sore, no insurance or stash for comfort,
all her savings locked into the house she knows she
won't be house-bound to, not that house-proud, a line
of steps stretching in front of her, block after block,
the miles adding up in her imagination, all those steps
she hadn't counted on, the cords in her calves growing
tauter and tauter until, all on their own, they begin
to vibrate with a song she hasn't heard for years,
thought she'd forgotten the words.

Madonna and child

Anne's son came up in the group of kids
at the biology camp. She told the other artists
she wouldn't make a fuss and she didn't, bit
her tongue when he didn't look her way
in the dining hall, held her tongue when she
saw him walk by with the girl. Hugs and kisses
on day one, out of sight, then just nods
as they pass on the path to the washrooms,
nothing said, the standoff understood. She wants
to tell him to wear a sweater at night
but she knows he'd pay a price in kidding
worse than any cold he might catch, so she just
nods, allows herself a wistful "Hi," but not so wistful
anyone might notice. One day fate conspires to have
them together in the food line, he's wearing
a sweatshirt she doesn't know and she's talking
to someone, distracted, and then there they
are, mother and son, about to take bread together
if not actually break it. She frowns at his plate, wants
to remind him about his veggies, but she keeps it
simple, "Have a good evening, sweetie," the last word
out before she can bite her lip. One of the girls
in cutoffs looks up and he hisses "It's Seth, Mom."
After supper, she walks down to the dock, gazes
into murky water. It's too early, but she imagines
she can hear the crying of the loons.

The heart in its nest
(for Mari-lou Rowley)

The bird you found on the trail, its wing
strong enough but its will broken, died
in the morning in the nest you'd made for it
from a computer box. Shut down, there was
nothing to do but dig a hole, shake out
the box. A neighbour identified it for you,
an evening grosbeak, and thought perhaps
it had hit a window as stupid birds
will sometimes do, had the wind knocked
out of it but no more, but there was
more. The bird had flapped like a moth
in a jar when you put your jacket
around it, and the thump
of its black and white wings
against your breasts as you lugged it home
made you think of your own heart, deeper
in, of the catheter and the laser gun
they'd threaded through your vein
to the thickened wall where one part of you
was always racing ahead of the rest, a child
so anxious to be home.

You couldn't help but think of yourself
every time you visited the bird, heard
its brave welcome, watched its frantic try
to stand, the legs more like rubber bands
than the broken twigs they resembled, and you
remembered the rubber in your own legs
after they wheeled you back to your room,
made you get up for a pee, get things moving
again. The doctors had apologized, said they
could try again in a year or two when
the technology had caught up, and you
could feel your heart leaping
ahead, another deadline to beat. There was
something broken inside the bird, your neighbour
said, something no amount of love or sugar water
could fix, no splint would set straight. He did
what had to be done while you looked
away, trying not to think of the flash
of yellow and listening to the murmuring
of your heart, and counting, counting.

War story

(for Esther)

On a rock by the pond
where snapping turtles took
the sun, my sister sat brushing
her hair and singing patriotic songs
softly to herself, one hundred strokes
with one hand, one hundred with
the other, *till Johnny comes marching*
home again hoorah hoorah. Her hair
in those days was long as willow branches
and sun-yellow, as yellow, our mother
used to say, as the yolk of an egg, dark yellow
with the implied blood of the birds
that would never fly. Her hair poured
off her serious narrow temples like the torrents
of hissing water I would see years later
at Niagara Falls, muscular rivulets of hair
racing itself down the rapids of her shoulders
to the calm at her waist, the long serene eddy
of her hips, not yet flared. As she brushed
and sang she dreamed of a boy who might run
his fingers roughly through her hair
and at that precise moment in Duluth, Minnesota,
just such a boy was stepping out of the darkness
of a movie theatre on State Street into the glare
of the late matinee sun, his fickle arm around
the waist of a girl he loved intently that moment
but would soon forget. Yes, these are
the characters and the end of chapter 1, oh,
and one other, a German boy, wiping sleep
from his eyes.

My sister ten, eleven, twelve, her arm
growing tired from the brushing, the boy
just turned eighteen and at boot camp, learning
to disassemble and clean his rifle with his eyes
closed, the way they'd been when he'd kissed
that other girl. The rifle a black glistening thing
filled with promise of noise and an ache
in his shoulder. His shooting at the range
always so good before, just off today
until the sergeant adjusted the sights
on the scope and saw the problem, the fine line
of the horizon where it crossed the upright arm
of the law smudged just so, a hair frayed
the way tempers of sergeants surely did, the way
patience does even now. My sister dreaming,
her hair squared at her shoulder blades, the yellow
already starting to fade, like wheat at the end
of a long summer. Did it hurt, I asked, and yes
it did, she said, but not the hair, laughing
at me, the little brother, well where then? Here,
she said, pointing to her heart. The hair
lovingly collected in twined strands, laid gently
in tissue paper and sent away, she said, to where
it would do the most good, the crosshairs
sharp as a barber's scissors today, the boy's shot
true, exploding the heart of that other boy, that boy
on the other side of the line, my sister dreaming, singing
johnny come marching home again, the snapping turtles
sensing the menace in her and diving deep,
deep.

Mona Lisa, 1998

(for Jennifer Sloan)

Beneath soft hair and the smooth curve
of temple, the devious brain ticks, a grid
of steel enmeshing thought. Behind
serene eyes, a rusted coil pulsing
with the sad echo of motion. Behind
the fine curved nose, a mouse trap
waiting to spring. And the smile, ah,
beneath that smile – glittering teeth
pronouncing your name.

The beautiful wives

"And wives, the beautiful wives in the stands now
take the interest they once feigned, oh, long ago, their
marriages just begun.... The wives, the beautiful wives
are with their men."
— Richard Hugo, "Missoula Softball Tournament"

The beautiful wife is packing her bag
in the basement where whatever noise
she makes won't carry. She is surrounded
here by moments in her life as a wife, the head
of a deer she cried over every time the steaks
came out of the freezer, the bowling trophies
and the large-screen TV, an empty golfbag
crumpled and dejected as a spent scrotum. In
the wavy mirror over the wetbar her fading beauty
is so obvious she could cry except she has no tears
left, she has held on as long as she could, for the children,
for her mother's pride, to spite what her father
forecast, for what she thought was her own pride
except now she knows she is moving toward it, not
away. But this is not a poem as you might expect
of the battered wife, the abused wife, the wife
ignored or scorned. It is a poem of the beautiful wife
alone in the stands with the singing of the national anthem
still buzzing in her ears, all its promise, the tears
it can bring choked back as she watches in the dusty light
of distance her man walk slowly to the plate.

Again the orchard

The dimensions of an orchard
are the length of a woman's reach
by the breadth of her desire. On all sides
there are barriers, injunctions. Good fences
do not necessarily make good neighbours
but good vantage points from which to see
the way you might have wished
to have come, the way you might some day
still go, given the chance. You are a stranger
in your own home, unable to speak
the language of your family. They turn to you
with looks of surprise and disappointment
and it's true that you have gone against
their wish for good order, all the proportions
of the peaceable garden they had every right
to expect. There is a cornucopia of fruit
and only one with blandishments, yet
it is that one which undulates through
your dreams, the absence of its shape
in your mouth haunting your hunger, its
imagined taste corroding your tongue.
Eventually, the dimensions of an orchard
confine a woman, suffocate her. They are
both too large and too small for her imagination
to encompass. With no way out, she can
only hope to climb.